Ghosts of Bed

A play

Arthur Aldrich

Samuel French — London
www.samuelfrench-london.co.uk

GHOSTS OF BEDLAM

First produced at Leicestershire Drama Festival on 13th April, 1991, with the following cast of characters.

Janet Crawford	Maggie Law
Rachel Walters	Jenny Phipps
Royston Chatsworth	Wayne Jennings
Milly	Kate Bishop

Directed by Peter Brine (for "Plaudite")

CHARACTERS

Janet Crawford, a caretaker in her fifties
Rachel Walters, a civil servant in her thirties
Royston Chatsworth, a documentary film-maker in his late forties
Milly, a tramp and former mental patient

The action takes place in a ward of a former mental hospital

Time—the later years of the twentieth century

Also by Arthur Aldrich, published by Samuel French

Housewarming
Road to Northborough
Shindig

GHOSTS OF BEDLAM

The ward of a former mental hospital

Built in Victorian times, the hospital was taken out of use in the nineteen eighties. The ward is empty , except for one bed upstage, complete with mattress, pillow and blankets piled on it. There are two archways at either side of the stage, leading into corridors, which are in darkness. The only windows, which can be suggested by lighting, are high up at ceiling height. There is a naked light bulb and a few broken fittings

The Lights come up. Janet Crawford, in a scruffy overall and carrying a large bunch of keys, enters R. She is a caretaker in her fifties. Following closely is Rachel Walters, a civil servant in her thirties. She wears a smart suit and carries a document case

Janet Or there's this one. Simkins Ward where they used to put the long-term cases. Wall to wall bedsteads. The smell of piss was something awful.

Rachel (*sniffing*) It still is.

Janet And that's your lot!

Rachel Incredibly dirty, all of it.

Janet Ah well. I'm only the caretaker. Cleaners cost extra.

Rachel Still, for our purposes, a bit of dirt is all to the good. Now then, where's our great film producer? Never around when he's wanted.

Janet He turned right, when we turned left. Probably never see him again. This film you're making …

Rachel Might be making.

Janet What's it about?

Rachel Classified info, Mrs. Crawford. You'll be told all you need to know in due course.

Janet What's in it for me?

Rachel I beg your pardon?

Janet Miss Walters, I used to be a nurse here. Now I'm the caretaker. You can get blood out of a nurse, but not out of a caretaker. Know what I mean?

Rachel You're paid a wage. That covers all eventualities.

Royston Chatsworth enters R. *He is a documentary film-maker in his late forties and is dressed casually*

Royston Ah, there you are! Good God, what's the smell?

Rachel Don't ask.

Slight pause as Royston looks around

What do you think?

Royston Have we been here before?

Rachel No, Royston. We've been to just about everywhere else. But not here.

Royston Strange! I could have sworn. (*Shaking his head*) No, can't be. (*Pointing* L) What's through there?

Janet Stables!

Royston Pardon?

Janet Small rooms for private patients.

Rachel What are you talking about?

Janet Just a little joke. Rich loonies don't mix with poor loonies. The stables were where we put the awkward sods ——

Royston You mean this was a … ?

Janet Mental hospital, yes.

Royston So that's why … (*He stops. Turning to Rachel*) You didn't tell me.

Rachel It's not relevant.

Royston Oh yes, it is.

Rachel Can't see why.

Royston What was it like, Mrs. Crawford — in its heyday?

Janet Crowded, dirty and cold, if you must know. Patients kept running away and the staff, who went to look for them, mostly didn't bother to come back. Otherwise it was perfect.

Royston So you weren't sorry to see the place closed down?

Janet Closed down is it? As far as I'm concerned it's just empty of patients.

Royston Isn't that the same thing?

Janet We were told it was going to be turned into a modern psychiatric unit, to treat the people we'd just tossed back into the world. Right, Miss Walters?

Rachel Sorry — not my department!

Janet No, that was just bullshit to make us all go quietly.

Royston All except you?

Janet I'm part of the fixtures and fittings. Thirty years as an auxiliary. I couldn't face moving somewhere different. They wanted a caretaker and here I am. Now me and the ghosts are waiting for the bulldozers, aren't we, Miss Walters?

Rachel Mrs Crawford, there's no point in angling for information. I can't tell you what I don't know.

Royston There must be a lot of ghosts in a building like this.

Rachel Royston, will this place do or not?

Pause as Royston continues to look around

Only if it won't, we'll have to go somewhere else and that takes time. And I did tell you that I'm taking Mother to the theatre tonight and, if I'm late for that, my life won't be worth living.

Royston All right, Rachel, relax! You'll get your film.

Rachel Yes but when? And at what cost?

Royston This place makes me uneasy. It may do perfectly well, I don't know. Just give me time to work it out. OK?

Rachel I'm going to lunch. There's a public house in the village. I'll be in the lounge bar if you need me.

Royston Which I will — sooner or later.

Rachel Precisely.

Royston What about you, Mrs Crawford?

Janet The name's Janet and I sit in my little room and eat my sarnies.

Royston Will you stay and talk?

Janet If you like.

Rachel She'll have to show me the way out first.

Royston Ask the ghosts, Rachel. They'll direct you.

Janet Don't you believe it! This place is such a rabbit warren even they get lost. Come on, Miss Walters, I'll take you to the main staircase. After that, you keep turning left.

Janet goes out R

Rachel (*following Janet*) I'll see you later, Royston.

Rachel goes out R

Royston moves around, looking at the space from different angles. From his pocket he takes a small dictaphone, switches it on and speaks into it

Royston "Then and Now", film one. I think we've found somewhere, Valerie. It's not ideal but it'll have to do. Our Civil Servant is getting very tetchy and I can't afford to risk a cancellation. So the first problem will be the lighting. Get in touch with Gerry and find out if he's free for a meet on Friday. He may have some ideas. No real windows, that's … (*He breaks off because, in his wanderings, he has ended up near the archway* L)

There appears to be a figure standing in the darkness L, *which vanishes quickly*

Royston does a double-take but the figure has gone

Janet enters R *and stands watching him*

(*Peering into the darkness*) Hallo! Anyone there? It's all right, I won't … (*He shakes his head, uncertain whether he saw anyone or not. Into the dictaphone*) Valerie, this place is spooky. (*Pause*) Second problem … beds. We shall need about forty of them — hospital beds — you know the sort of thing.

Janet (*interrupting*) You wouldn't be talking to yourself now, would you?

Royston (*laughing*) Just recording a few impressions. Getting the ghosts on record. (*He switches off the dictaphone*)

Janet Made your day, didn't it, dearie — the thought of this place being haunted.

Royston Well ... it feels more like I'm being haunted.

Janet Who by? Miss Walters?

Royston Yes ... her as well.

Janet This film you're making — what's it about?

Royston That's an official secret.

Janet I'm an official. You can tell me.

Royston Miss Walters has forbidden me to tell anyone.

Janet (*sneering*) Miss Walters! She's just a junior Civil Servant. You're not frightened of her, are you?

Royston (*after a slight pause*) Well, between you and me, it's a documentary film entitled "Then and Now". It's to show how things were in hospitals ... what ... ten, fifteen years ago; and how much they've changed.

Janet Oh yes, they've changed all right. Empty wards, hospitals closed ...

Royston Not exactly that.

Janet People thrown out into the streets.

Royston No, no ... the buildings — Victorian, dirty, oppressive, overcrowded ...

Janet (*suspiciously*) Yes ...

Royston Should've been knocked down decades ago.

Janet Definitely.

Royston And replaced by modern concoctions of glass, concrete and air-conditioning. The aim of the film is to show how conditions have changed. How they've improved.

Janet (*angrily*) Nothing changes, Mr Chatsworth!

Royston (*taken aback*) Call me, Royston ... please.

Janet And there's a drawback to every so-called improvement. Don't you believe otherwise! (*She pauses*) Would you like me to explain?

Royston No, thanks. I really don't have much time.

Janet You don't look like a person who believes in fairy tales.

Royston When I make films for these people I don't ask whether they're fact or fiction.

Janet Then you should! People like you — clever people — have a responsibility to the rest of us to tell ——

Royston (*interrupting*) Janet, I am responsible to my bank manager and my family, in that order.

Janet And you're happy with that, are you, making money filming lies?

Royston Happiness doesn't come into it, I simply cannot afford to turn down work.

Janet I wonder what the ghosts will make of your little film. I think it's time you met one.

Royston Pardon?

Janet Ghosts! There's usually one around.

Royston I'm not in the mood for games.

Janet crosses to the archway L

Janet (*calling out*) Come along, Milly, you've been rumbled.

Milly peers from the darkness L. She is a tramp, dirty rather than ragged, with little distinction between flesh and clothing

Janet turns back to Royston. As she does so, Milly hobbles across to the bed, lies down and pulls a blanket over her head

When the patients left here — back into community care it was called — a lot of them, like Milly, ended up on the streets. (*Calling back over her shoulder*) I can see you, you old crow! (*To Royston*) Milly was here for fifteen years. She and the others don't know anywhere else, so they come back to haunt the old place. How they get in beats me, but I seem to spend half my working day turfing them out. Come and meet her! Only take a tip — breathe through your mouth.

Royston What?

Janet Your mouth! You'll see.

They both cross to Milly. Janet pulls back the blanket

Milly (*snarling*) Why can't you leave a body alone? (*She snatches the blanket from Janet*)

Janet You're persistent, Milly. I'll say that for you.

Janet pulls Milly to her feet

Come on, on your feet!

Royston suddenly turns aside and retches

I did warn you. Breathe through your mouth! You didn't have an early morning shower, Milly. I can tell.

Milly 'Ad a bath!

Janet When was that, last Christmas? (*To Royston*) You all right?

Royston (*gulping air*) Yes, yes, I'm sorry.

Milly 'As he got my money?

Janet Not today, Milly.

Milly I was robbed. They took my savings. I trusted 'em. Went to the police but they didn't wanna know. I could tell you 'bout it.

Janet You already have — over and over.

Milly No money?

Janet shakes her head

Then why's he 'ere?

Janet This is Royston, Milly. He's here to make a film.

Milly A real film? Like in the pictures? I saw lots of them. People in love. It were good.

Royston It's not that sort of film, Milly. It's a documentary — about the hospital.

Janet Don't you get lying to her! She's confused enough already.

Milly I'd like to be in a film.

Royston Now there's a thought.

Janet Miss Walters would never allow it. It'd spoil the fairy story.

Royston Perhaps if we were to clean her up a bit …

Janet How it was and how it is, Royston. No cheating!

Milly I could be a film star.

Janet Tell him what it was like when you first came here, Milly.

Pause. Milly looks from one to the other

Milly Well … we always 'ad cakes for tea. And lots of birthday parties. All my friends were 'ere. I can't remember all their … except Tom. He was my favourite, Tom. And Gladys — used to wee wee all over the place so they locked her up — (*whispering loudly*) — in the stables.

Royston Were you happy here, Milly?

Milly (*shaking her head but saying*) … Yes.

Janet Why shouldn't she be? She was safe; she had friends. Not many friends out there.

Milly I wasn't always like this you know.

Royston No. No, of course you weren't.

Milly When I was a little girl, we lived in a big house with a bathroom and a proper lavatory. I 'ad a different frock for all the days of the week. Then George came and took me away.

Royston Who was George?

Milly I loved 'im, he was little and he drunk beer. And 'e made me laugh.

Janet She says George was her husband.

Milly 'Usband yes. Mum died and I should've been rich. There was only me and that big 'ouse. They told me I was ill. You can't look after yourself, they kept saying … on and on at me. My kids didn't want to know and George was always … (*shouting suddenly*) … stinkin', bloody drunk. He knew, he knew. He stole my money.

Janet All right, Milly, calm down!

Royston Did anyone follow up this story?

Janet We're nurses, Royston, not debt collectors. Look, somewhere there's a husband but he never came near this place. Doubtful if the children, the house or the money ever existed. Once she was here, she invented a past that was probably in her dreams. Who are we to destroy that? So she's a fraud as well, aren't you, you old crow?

Milly (*tugging at Royston's sleeve*) George made me sign a bit of paper. I didn't know anything about the money. I never saw it again.

Royston Money's not everything, Milly.

Milly Yes, it bloody is.

Janet The fact is she needs care and attention. And there are hundreds like her, living in doorways, eating from other people's dustbins. You tell me how your film is going to help people like them.

Milly (*stroking Royston's face*) He's an 'andsome boy, ain't he! Mother's pride.

Royston tries to back away but Milly has him by the wrist

Janet (*laughing*) She's making you part of the family.

Royston It's very nice of you, Milly, but no thanks ——

Janet What's the matter, Royston? Smell got to your conscience, has it?

Milly continues to stroke his face

Royston Just get her off me, will you!

Milly They went away. Never even came to say goodbye. All I ever wanted — to see him again — just once. He was 'andsome. It would've made the others jealous. (*A sudden angry outburst*) But you didn't come. You didn't come to see me. And now it's too bloody late.

And she beats him with her fists. Royston backs away. Janet moves quickly to quieten Milly

Janet Eh … eh, Milly! (*She envelops her in her arms*) Calm down now, girl! Calm down!

Royston God, she's mad!

Janet Precisely. You hungry, Milly?

Milly Always 'ungry.

Janet Go and wait by my room and I'll make you some soup. (*She releases her*)

Milly What sort?

Janet (*shooing her away*) Go on, away with you! What sort of soup! Soupy soup, that's what.

Milly goes out R

Milly (*as she goes*) Only you know I 'ate tomato soup. I 'ate tomatoes as well.

Slight pause. Royston looks embarrassed

Janet You all right?

Royston She er … she took me by surprise.

Janet Sundays used to be the day when all the sane people came to visit the insane. I found it almost impossible to tell them apart. What about you, Royston?

Royston Well! … I suppose we can all be a bit odd at times.

Janet As odd as Milly? What do you suggest we do about her?

Royston Don't ask me. I'm not a doctor.

Janet Should we lock her up or set her free? (*Pause*) Come on, Royston, you've met her, you've talked to her. What do you think?

Royston I suppose she should be looked after somewhere.

Janet In a place like this?

Royston Somewhere better if possible.

Janet Or should we just ignore them and hope they'll go away. 'Cause looking after people costs money.

Royston I know that. I'll pay my share. Now if you'll excuse me, Janet, I have a film to make.

Janet (*interrupting*) You'll pay your share but will you play your part? You're the film-maker.

Royston Janet, I'm sorry for Milly and all the others like her. But I can't solve the problems of the nation's health in one little documentary.

Janet Shame! Such a good opportunity. What happens then? After you've filmed this place?

Royston We go and take pretty pictures of a new one.

Janet Oh yes, I bet Miss Walters found you somewhere really tasty.

Royston She did actually. Brand new. Not opened yet.

Janet I know. A glass and concrete hotel where the central heating costs more than a nurse's yearly wage.

Royston I thought you wanted modern hospitals.

Janet Sure! But there's more to it than that. We hated this place — the dirt, the cold, the leaky roof. And above all the smell. But it worked. We made it work. It was home, sweet home for a lot of disturbed people.

Royston I'm not sure you know what you do want.

Janet I want …(*she pauses*) … a few accurate pictures and some truthful words.

Royston shrugs his shoulders

I mean, what is it with you people? If it were starving children or animals being ill-treated, you'd be taking pictures by the million. A football club about to go bankrupt and the words pour out in torrents. But lunatics turned out for care in the community and buildings like this being demolished to make way for some rich man's development, instead of being repaired and improved, and suddenly there's total silence. Why?

Royston I don't know. People aren't interested, I suppose.

Janet Bullshit! They're not being told. You tell stories with pictures. Tell a real story for a change.

Royston Not me, Janet. Not this time!

Janet Why not, for Christ's sake? What's bugging you?

Royston I couldn't begin to tell you.

Janet All right, make your film! But don't get any romantic ideas. This place was sheer bedlam in its time. Screams and smells! Always the smell. Can you get that into your camera?

Royston (*laughing uneasily*) It'd probably rot the film.

Janet You can't escape, you know. Ask Milly! When she lived here, she was always running away. Now she's free, she keeps coming back. That's madness. (*She moves away*) I'll leave you to get on.

Royston Thanks. I'll see you before I go.
Janet I shall expect a good tip.

Janet exits R

Royston stands for a moment, looking around then he takes out and switches on his dictaphone

Royston Valerie … this is not going to be easy. Never mind the technical details, there's a caretaker here — an ex-nurse — who doesn't approve of what we're doing. Not so sure I approve myself. The problem is — the problem is … God knows I try to take an impersonal view of my work but this place … it's opened the door on a few memories, I can tell you. Bad memories. (*He pauses to peer through the archway* L) I can't get out of my mind a small room at the end of a long corridor — like a stable, with a split door. And freezing cold, with bars at the broken window. And someone lying on a bed under hessian sheets. Can you imagine it? I can and I wish I couldn't.
Janet (*off*) Mr Chatsworth! Mr Chatsworth, are you there?
Royston Hang on, I'm coming!

He switches off his dictaphone and goes out R

The Lights become brighter and sunnier

Janet enters R, *now in her auxiliary nurse's uniform. She is carrying a wicker chair, which she places* C. *She goes back to the entrance*

Janet (*calling off*) Mr Chatsworth! (*Pause*) Mr Chatsworth!

Royston enters R. *He is wearing a tie and jacket*

Ah, there you are! You can wait here, Mr Chatsworth. It's nice and quiet. But you may be in for a long wait.
Royston Oh, why's that? (*He sits*)

Janet We've mislaid her, that's why. Oh, it's nothing to worry about. The search parties are out. She'll turn up

Royston Shouldn't you … I mean … don't you keep tabs on the patients?

Janet We do our best, Mr Chatsworth. But she's not one of those under lock and key. Your mother's taken to going on shopping expeditions into town.

Royston Is that safe?

Janet We don't encourage it. We did think we'd found a solution but she's a very determined lady.

Royston You ought to do something. I mean … it's a very busy road out there. She could be …

Milly enters L, *now as Millicent, with a clean face and wearing a dress and cardigan. Tied to her rear quarters is another wicker chair, which she carries without any obvious difficulty, apart from a slightly uneven gait*

Janet Well, look who it isn't!

Milly sits herself down next to Royston

Where do you think you've been, you naughty girl?

Royston (*kissing Milly*) Hallo, Mother.

Janet We tied you down in that chair to stop you running away. Fat lot of use!

Milly The shops were shut but there was a wedding in the church. And a road accident. Are you my boy?

Royston Yes, Mother.

Milly Where's your pretty girl-friend? I like her. Have you brought me any chocolate?

Royston No, I'm sorry, I haven't.

Milly stands, chair still attached

Milly You're a big disappointment to me. Why aren't you wearing your uniform?

Royston I left the army a year ago, Mother.

Milly I'm going for a walk. (*She heads upstage*)

Janet (*pursuing her*) Oh no, you're not. We've wasted enough time this afternoon looking for you.

Janet turns Milly round and leads her downstage

And my time is money.

Milly If I had money, I could cure my headaches.

Janet And I've another bone to pick with you, my girl.

Milly No, I don't think I'll stay here. (*She turns around and scuttles back upstage*)

Janet (*pulling her back*) Come back!

Milly You're hurting.

Royston Mother, please do as you're told.

Janet pushes Milly into a sitting position

Janet Who ripped up their sheets last night?

Royston Oh Mother, not again!

Milly It wasn't me. I didn't! I didn't!

Janet You know what happens to naughty girls who rip up their sheets. They have to go back into the stables.

Milly You don't frighten me, you ogre. And I want my tea. I want my tea.

Janet You see what it's like, Mr Chatsworth. People have no idea what goes on in here.

Royston No, I don't suppose they do.

Janet What do you do for a living?

Royston I've just started at the *Evening News* as a reporter.

Janet Oh, that's nice. Of course we're so short-handed we can't really nurse them properly. And half of them shouldn't be in here — work-shy malingerers — as normal as you and me. Not your mother, of course. She's a pleasure to look after — when she's behaving herself that is, and not running away.

Royston I'm sorry about that.

Janet Not your fault, dear. But it'd make a good article for your newspaper. Life inside the asylum. That'd open people's eyes.

Royston Actually we tend to concentrate on births, deaths and marriages. Local events, you know.

Janet Pity! 'Cause a bit of interest from newspapers would be a great help.

Royston (*looking around*) It can't be a very pleasant place to work.

Janet It's prehistoric, Mr Chatsworth. I wish a bloody great wind'd blow it away. And then we could have a new building and new attitudes. We'd also like to have central heating.

Milly And I'd like to have my tea.

Janet Yes. Well you'll have to wait, won't you? I'm going to prepare your new room — in the stables.

Royston Does she have to go back there?

Janet Sister's decision. But she's better off on her own, in the circumstances.

Milly Nurse! Nurse!

Janet What now?

Milly I've got the wrong teeth.

Janet Let me see!

Milly That Tom was round here yesterday. Oh he's a lad! Stealing things, mixing things up.

Janet (*taking Milly by the chin*) They look all right to me.

Milly I tell you — they're the wrong teeth.

Janet You'll survive.

Janet lets go of Milly, turns and exits L

Royston Mum, are you sure?

Milly I know my own teeth. These don't feel right.

Royston Well — well what do you do with them? How come they go missing?

Milly Where's that girl you married? I liked her.

Royston I'm not married. Just tell me about those teeth!

Milly But you will be a good boy and marry her, won't you?

Royston If you mean Penny, I'm not going out with her any more.

Milly Not like that rascal Tom. Do you know, some nights he tries to get into my bed. I shout out but no-one takes any notice.

Royston Mum, what are you …?

Milly He wants to marry, me.

Royston Hang on — what are you saying?

Milly He wants my hand in marriage. Do you think your father will mind?

Royston No, no — about him trying to get into your bed.

Milly I tell him, it's mine. You go to your own bed.

Royston Are you telling me the truth?

Milly Don't be angry. I told them … I did … I told them, I'll sleep with my teeth in. But they won't let us. They — they take them out of our mouths and put them in a bowl of water — all mixed up.

Royston But surely the nurses … (*He stands*). I don't know what to believe. I'll go and have a word. (*He moves away from her*)

Milly Why are you frightened of me, Royston?

Royston (*turning*) Don't be daft, Mum. I'm not frightened.

Milly When I go for a walk, people point at me and children laugh and throw things. They're frightened, I know they are.

Royston You musn't take any notice.

Milly And you musn't either. When they point at you.

Royston No-one points at me.

Milly You're the son of a mad woman.

Royston I wish you wouldn't talk like that.

Milly It must be a secret, Royston — a secret between you and me. It's my birthday next week.

Royston I haven't forgotten.

Milly (*clutching at him*) Take me home, Royston! Take me home!

Royston (*sitting next to her*) Mum, I will. I will take you home — just as soon as you're better.

Milly Better! Better than what, boy? How can I be better? I've been good all my life. I want to go home now.

Royston Mum, I can't! I mean, how can I? I don't have the time. How can I look after you?

Milly I look after myself.

Royston Yes — like you did before.

Milly I'm clean, I use the toilet properly, when they let me. I don't like it here. I want to go home.

Royston You can't, Mum, so don't ask!

Milly You must help me. They're cruel … and rough … and dirty.
Some of them … (*confidentially*) … some of them are not right
in the head. What am I doing here, boy? Tell me that! I don't
belong here. They say they're going to cure me but I already am.
I sit for hours and nothing happens. No-one comes and asks me
how I am. No doctors, no nurses, not even family.

Royston I'm family. I'm always asking.

Milly I'm lonely. And cold. At nights I'm cold — in that room. I
don't sleep. I make things instead — bandages — long white
bandages. But no-one ever says thank you. They lock me in. I look
at them and I know — I know I don't belong here. I'm in prison,
boy. You will rescue me, won't you?

Royston (*standing*) Mum, I can't look after you. I'm not qualified
and I don't have the time. Besides I can't give up work.

Royston goes out L

Milly (*calling after him*) I'll die here if no-one rescues me. (*Quietly*)
I'll die here.

*The Lights dim, leaving Milly and the wicker chairs in a spotlight.
Offstage party music starts: "The Teddy Bears' Picnic". The Lights
come up to full*

Janet and Royston enter L. *They are both wearing party hats and
Janet carries a bedpan, tied with a ribbon*

Janet Here she is … here's the birthday girl!

Milly Go away!

The music fades down to background

Royston (*kissing Milly*) Happy Birthday, Mother.

Milly (*squirming in the chair*) I don't know you. Leave me alone!

Janet Who's a grumpy girl then?

Milly You'd be grumpy if they gave you boiled cabbage every day.

Royston (*putting a paper hat on her head*) Cabbage is good for you.

Milly If it's my birthday, why didn't you bring me a present?
Royston I've brought you some flowers. I put them in your room.
Milly They'll get frostbite in there.

The music stops

Janet I've got a present for you. Here you are, Millicent. (*She offers her the bedpan*)
Milly I don't want that thing. I use a commode. I'd use a toilet if you'd let me.
Janet Pull the ribbon!
Milly And I went this morning, so I don't need to go again.
Royston Come on, Mother, it's your birthday. The nurses have gone to a lot of trouble.
Milly What sort of trouble? I'm no trouble.
Janet We're having a party for you, Millicent, on the veranda. All your friends will be there.
Milly Tom? Will Tom be there?
Janet Yes, Tom's there. And Ethel and Doris, George, Eric and Agnes, Fred and ——
Milly He tried to get into my bed again last night.
Royston Who did?
Milly He's a rascal, that Tom.
Janet Wishful thinking, Millicent.
Royston She told me that he proposed to her.
Janet It's possible. Doesn't mean anything. Proposing's the way his madness takes him.
Royston But he is ... well ... kept under control?
Janet Oh Tom's no problem. He's only five foot nothing. A pest, of course, and a tea leaf; so he has to be watched. But there's no real harm in him.
Royston (*doubtfully*) I mean there's no possibility ...
Janet Mr Chatsworth, what sort of ship do you think we run? This is a mental hospital. People imagine all sorts of things.
Royston Yes, I suppose so.
Janet Here, hold this!

Janet gives him the bedpan

> Come on, Millicent, your guests are waiting. (*She unties the rope holding Milly in the chair*) There'll be music and dancing and jellies and blancmange.

Milly And a cake?

Janet Yes … and a cake with candles for you to blow out.

Janet helps Milly to her feet

Milly What about my present?

Royston Come on, Mother, let's see what it is. Pull the ribbon!

Milly (*undoing the bow*) I love presents.

Royston And behold! (*He takes the lid off the bedpan and is surprised and disgusted by what he sees*)

Milly (*delighted*) You've found them, nurse. I knew you would. (*She takes a set of false teeth from the bedpan*)

Janet And do you know where I found them?

Royston Is this someone's idea of a joke?

Janet Teeth are no joke in this place, Mr Chatsworth. I found them in the broom cupboard. Now how did they get there, Millicent?

Milly It's that Tom. It's all right for him. You let him sleep with his teeth.

Janet Because they're his own, love. Part of his fixtures and fittings, he can't choke on them.

Royston Whose sick idea was it to put them in this?

Janet It's a joke, dear. Don't worry, it's been sterilized.

Royston She has a set of teeth already.

Janet But they're not hers. Hers are marked on the plate. Everyone knows Millicent's teeth. They've gone missing often enough.

Royston Then whose is she wearing?

Janet God knows.

Royston I ought to complain.

Janet (*shrugging*) We cling to little jokes like that in this place. Otherwise we'd go mad. Anyway she's glad to get them back, aren't you, Millicent?

Milly I knew you'd find them if you looked properly.

Janet Come on, love, pick up your chair and walk! (*Calling out*)
   Make way for the birthday girl.

Janet sings "Happy Birthday"

   *Meanwhile, Milly places her false teeth on the wicker chair and
   carries it and them in state from the ward, as she exits L*

*Janet takes the bedpan from Royston and, still singing, follows
Milly. In the archway she stops singing and turns*

   You as well, Mr Chatsworth. You're the guest of honour.

   Janet goes out

*Royston sits on the remaining chair and holds his head in his hands.
Off, "The Teddy Bears' Picnic" can be faintly heard*

   Janet returns after a moment

Janet Are you coming, Mr Chatsworth?
Royston In a minute.
Janet You don't enjoy visiting, do you?
Royston (*shaking his head*) It's all so — so degrading.
Janet For all of us. So you'd better get used to it.
Royston The doctor said he's going to try some different drugs.
Janet Don't build your hopes, Mr Chatsworth. Drugs, operations
   — it's all experimental. They don't really have a clue.
Royston How long do you think she'll be in here?
Janet Until someone comes up with a better way to deal with her
   sort of illness. Except I don't think they're trying too hard. It costs
   money. Of course she's a voluntary patient. You can take her
   home whenever you want.
Royston If you knew the trouble I had before …
Janet Oh I know. She's hard work. But she'll be happy here. So,
   on your feet, Mr Chatsworth, I need that chair.

He stands. She takes the chair and starts to leave

Royston Nurse! I er … I would just like to say — I do appreciate all you're doing for her.

Janet Yes, the world overflows with appreciation. But it doesn't get us very far. There's a party going on. Come and join us!

Janet goes out L, carrying the chair. Royston follows her

The Lights start to fade and the off stage music gets louder. Blackout and the music stops. Pause. The Lights come up slowly.

Royston, dressed as earlier, stands in the archway L. He moves C

Royston (*into the dictaphone*) So, Valerie, provided we can get hold of about forty beds and provided Gerry can solve the lighting, there shouldn't be any problem. Except … I'm beginning to wish I hadn't accepted this job. I could make up a story about this place; but it wouldn't please many people; and it wouldn't pay any money.

Janet, in her caretaker's overall, enters R. She is carrying a cup of soup

Janet I talk to myself a lot. If I had one of those things, it'd stop people jumping to the wrong conclusion.

Royston (*putting away the dictaphone*) Do they doubt you?

Janet Thirty years with the insane. I must be a bit touched, musn't I? (*Holding out the cup*) I thought you might like this.

Royston (*taking the cup*) Yeah, thanks.

Janet You all sorted then?

Royston I think so. We'll film in two weeks time. Should be in and out in a day. I promise not to make a mess.

Janet You'd better not.

Slight pause. Royston drinks his soup

Still the fairy tale I suppose?

Royston I don't have much alternative. The truth according to Miss
   Walters is set in concrete. One word out of place, one wrong
   picture and I'm sunk.

Janet Is that what you're frightened of — the sack?

Royston Not really. I've been there before.

Janet What then?

Royston Between you and me, Janet — ghosts!

Janet That was a joke, Royston. Milly's no ghost.

Royston She reminds me of one.

Janet Why's that?

Royston Oh, it's not important.

Janet Tell me about it.

Royston I've spent most of my life trying not to tell anyone.

Janet What's the point of that?

Royston It was all a long time ago. A small room with broken
   windows and hessian sheets on the bed. You'd know the sort of
   place.

Janet (*nodding*) Oh yes. Who was it? Someone close?

Royston That's one photograph I never took. (*Tapping his fore-
   head*) But it's up here all the same.

There is a loud shout off R

   Rachel Walters quickly enters R, *leading in by the arm a loudly
   protesting and once again scruffy Milly who is clutching a blanket*

Milly Sodding well let go of me! You're 'urting. (*She struggles*)

Rachel The pub food wasn't up to much so I came back early, only
   to find this — this tramp ——

Milly screeches

   Keep still! This tramp making off with stolen property.

Milly My blanket! I was give it.

Rachel Then give it back or we shall call the police.

Janet We're not having any police in here.

Milly Bastard!

Milly aims a kick at Rachel's shin, but Rachel leaps to one side, dropping her document case. She then twists Milly's arm up the middle of her back. Milly shouts in pain

Rachel Royston, don't just stand there! Get the blanket?
Royston Rachel, be reasonable.
Rachel Royston, come and help me! And you, Mrs Crawford!

Rachel twists Milly's arm again. Milly screams

Janet (*crossing to her*) Miss Walters, Milly sort of lives here. She's a harmless old lady and I won't stand by and watch her being mistreated. So — (*prodding Rachel as she speaks*) — kindly — let — her — go!
Rachel How dare you! Who do you think ——?
Janet (*continuing to prod*) Do — as — I — say.
Rachel I warn you, Mrs Crawford, I shall call the police and have you charged with assault.
Janet Do whatever you like but — (*more prodding*) — let — Milly — go!
Rachel Royston, please …!

But, seeing no help coming from Royston, Rachel, still holding Milly, tries to turn away and then suddenly retaliates by lashing out with her free hand, slapping Janet's face. Janet steps back, more in surprise than pain

Janet Right, if that's the way it's to be …

Fist clenched, Janet advances towards Rachel, who retreats, still holding on to Milly

Milly (*struggling*) Will you bloody let go of me!

Royston tries to intercept Janet

Royston Janet! Janet, don't!

Janet (*pushing him aside*) Stay out of this, Royston!
Royston It won't do any good.
Rachel Don't you dare, Mrs Crawford. I warn you …
Janet You started this.
Rachel All right, all right. I'm sorry ——

But Janet's fist is already on its way. Rachel sways to one side,
leaving Milly to catch the full force of the blow. Milly sinks to the
floor, dropping her blanket as she does so

Janet Milly!
Royston God, I hate violence …
Rachel Now look what you've done.
Janet (*kneeling beside Milly*). Milly! Come on, you old crone,
wake up!

No response from Milly

(*Standing*) I'll get the first aid. Royston, keep that one —
(*pointing to Rachel*) — away from her.

Janet hurries out

Rachel Oh God, what a day! You might've turned in a better
performance.
Royston I couldn't possibly compete with you. (*Kneeling beside*
Milly) Milly, can you hear me?
Rachel Theft, trespass and common assault. Don't they mean
anything to you?
Royston In these circumstances not a lot!

Milly stirs and opens her eyes

Milly? Milly, are you all right?
Milly 'Course I'm bloody not! I was 'it!
Rachel Takes more than a cuff round the ear to hurt people like her.
Milly Keep her away from me. She's mad.

Royston Calm down, Milly.

Janet returns with a first-aid box and a glass of water

Janet How is she? (*Kneeling beside Milly*) Milly … come on, gal, drink this!

Milly Don't want no medicine!

Janet It's only water.

Milly Don't want bloody water neither! Want money! Help me up!

Janet Royston, give me a hand, will you!

They help Milly to her feet

Better sit her down for a minute or two.

They help her across to the bed and she sits

Milly Haven't you got any … you know … any brandy or whisky or nothing?

Janet Water, Milly.

Milly Ugh! In the good old days, when we fell over, you always gave us a nip of brandy. Sometimes we used to fall over on purpose.

Janet Yeah, well them days are gone.

Rachel You're very foolish to keep encouraging these vagrants.

Janet You still here, Miss Walters? If I were you, I'd go quietly,

Rachel If you take my advice ——

Janet (*turning to her*) No thanks! You listen instead. Something I've learnt from thirty years of looking after these people. None of us are safe from something up here going snap. We're all potential Millys. And that includes you, Miss Walters.

Pause. Rachel stares at her, then turns away

Rachel I shall have to report this incident of course.

Janet Please yourself,

Rachel (*picking up the blanket*) And I'll take this as evidence.

Milly My blanket! I wan' it.

Janet Now that was a stupid thing to do.

Rachel If there's anyone who's been stupid, Mrs Crawford, I'd say it was you. As you will find out.

Janet You see, you might get away with holding Milly by the arm if you're very careful. But you won't get away with clutching that blanket to your chest.

Rachel What are you talking about? This is NHS property.

Janet I'm talking about fleas, Miss Walters. Milly's infested.

Rachel God!! (*She drops the blanket and beats at her clothes with her hands*) You might've told me.

Janet I'd've thought you'd have guessed about Milly's little friends.

Rachel Smelly little tramp! (*She removes her jacket and shakes it*)

Janet She was a patient in one of your hospitals. She didn't have fleas then. They were a welcoming present from the outside world. (*She picks up the blanket and crosses to Milly*) Here you are, Milly.

Milly (*clutching the blanket*) My blanket.

Rachel I'm not stopping here any longer, Royston.

Royston You go. I'll get a taxi into town.

Rachel We'll meet at my office in the morning.

Royston Er — no, I don't think so.

Rachel There's a lot to talk about. The filming schedule for a start.

Royston No. No, there isn't going to be any filming.

Rachel You needn't worry about Mrs Crawford. She won't ... (*She stops*) What did you say?

Royston No film, Rachel.

Janet Careful, Royston.

Rachel What do you mean, no film?

Royston Not from me. I can't find anywhere suitable.

Rachel You have to do it. You're under contract.

Royston I'll get a doctor's note. Save us all a lot of embarrassment.

Rachel But you can't just give up, not at this stage. You can't! Now look, Royston, we've always worked so well together. And — and what about the expense? I mean, we've travelled half way round the country for this. We've had our disagreements in the past, I know, but things've worked out. And that business just now, it's not important. Just my bad temper. Oh, God, what will the office say?

Royston I shan't speak out of turn if that's what you're worried about.

Rachel Why, Royston? Why?

Royston I'm glad you brought me here. It's brought me face to face with a few ghosts.

Rachel Ghosts!

Royston Personal ghosts, Rachel. Even you must have a few of those.

Rachel If I have, I don't let them interfere with my work.

Royston What you're trying to do here, what we all try to do, is create illusions. I take pretty pictures where the sun is always shining. That's not reality. It never was, or is, or will be. My ghosts are more real; Milly's real; thinking blankets are more important than human beings, that's real. And I don't want to be part of it any more.

Rachel Thank you for that character reference.

Royston It's not personal, Rachel. But even you must realize there has to be a different way to treat … people like Milly.

Rachel My … our department doesn't create these people you know. We're just left to deal with them. We're supposed to brush them under the carpet so that the public's conscience isn't troubled. And that's not easy because they're always with us.

Milly is closely examining her blanket

And no matter how many changes we make, things never seem to improve. Can you think of a solution? Because, if you can, feel free! In the meantime, don't sacrifice me to your ghosts. I'm merely doing the job I'm paid for — part of a problem, for which we're all …

Rachel sees Milly approaching

… all responsible.

Milly I've found one. Would you like to see it?

Rachel No! No, thank you very much. You keep it. (*She moves to leave. Turning*). In fact, as far as I'm concerned, you can keep the whole bloody place.

Rachel goes out R

Janet I think that puts us both out of work.

Royston Pretty futile gesture, wasn't it?

Janet Oh yes, won't solve a thing. Hardly a ripple.

Royston All right, Janet, you tell me. What do I have to do?

Janet Well, for a start, you could let Milly live next door to you.

Royston (*laughing*) The neighbours wouldn't like that.

Janet Exactly! So don't bother their sane, little heads. And, as for this and all our other ghosts, close down and move on. You all right, Milly?

Milly Didn't like 'er. She took my blanket.

Janet You got off lightly, Milly. You'll have to stay away from here. She'll be back on her bulldozer to get revenge. Still, I'm grateful to you, Royston. I'd rather the old place was knocked down than lied about. (*She pauses*) Shall I 'phone for a taxi?

Royston Yes, please.

Janet goes out R

Royston takes out his dictaphone, switches it on and talks into it. Milly watches him.

Royston Valerie — "Then and Now", Film one is cancelled. The whole project is cancelled. Sorry to tell you but we're both out of work again. I'll explain later.

Milly (*holding out her hand*) Me! Me!

Royston (*holding out the dictaphone*) Say hallo to Valerie.

Milly (*shouting*) Hallo, Valerie! Have you got my money? (*And she cackles loudly*)

Royston That was Milly. She's out of work as well. Listen, get in touch with Paul at Mountfield Productions — see if he's free for lunch sometime soon. I've an idea for a story that might interest him. Social problem, tell him. He likes that sort of thing. Besides, I have to make a crust best way I can. I'll leave this on your desk tonight and give you a bell tomorrow afternoon. *Ciao*! (*He switches off the dictaphone and puts it into his pocket*)

Milly Who is it?

Royston My secretary. I'm going now, Milly. I hope they find you somewhere ... no, I hope you get your money — lots of it. That's all that matters nowadays. 'Bye! (*He starts to go*)

Milly Mister!

Royston turns

I like you, Mister. Take me home!

Royston Oh Milly, don't ask!

Royston goes out R

Milly Take me home, Mister! Take me home!

She stands C, *hugging her blanket*

BLACK-OUT

FURNITURE AND PROPERTY LIST

On stage: Bed. *On it*: mattress, pillow, blanket

Off stage: Large bunch of keys (**Janet**)
Document case (**Rachel**)
Wicker chair (**Janet**)
Bedpan tied with a ribbon and containing set of false teeth
    (**Janet**)
Paper party hat (**Royston**)
Cup of soup (**Janet**)
Blanket (**Milly**)
First-aid box, glass of water (**Janet**)

Personal: **Royston**: dictaphone in pocket
Milly: wicker chair

LIGHTING PLOT

Property fittings required: naked pendant lightbulb
Interior. The same scene throughout

To open: Sombre general lighting

Cue 1	**Royston** goes out R *Increase to bright sunny effect*	(Page 12)
Cue 2	**Milly**: "I'll die here." *Fade to spotlight on* **Milly**	(Page 17)
Cue 3	Music starts *Bring up lighting to bright sunny effect*	(Page 17)
Cue 4	**Royston** follows **Janet** off *Fade to black-out; when ready, slowly bring up sombre general lighting as at opening*	(Page 21)
Cue 5	**Milly** stands C, hugging her blanket *Black-out*	(Page 29)

EFFECTS PLOT

Printed by The Kingfisher Press, London NW10 7AS